SKILLS OF AN EFFECTIVE ADMINISTRATOR

Harvard Business Review
C L A S S I C S

SKILLS OF AN EFFECTIVE ADMINISTRATOR

Robert L. Katz

Harvard Business Press
Boston, Massachusetts

THE HARVARD BUSINESS REVIEW CLASSICS SERIES

Since 1922, *Harvard Business Review* has been a leading source of breakthrough ideas in management practice—many of which still speak to and influence us today. The HBR Classics series now offers you the opportunity to make these seminal pieces a part of your permanent management library. Each volume contains a groundbreaking idea that has shaped best practices and inspired countless managers around the world—and will change how you think about the business world today.

SKILLS OF AN EFFECTIVE ADMINISTRATOR

Although the selection and training of good administrators is widely recognized as one of American industry's most pressing problems, there is surprisingly little agreement among executives or educators on what makes a good administrator. The executive development programs of some of the nation's leading corporations and colleges reflect a tremendous variation in objectives.

At the root of this difference is industry's search for the traits or attributes which will objectively identify the "ideal executive" who is equipped to cope effectively with any problem in any organization. As one observer of U.S. industry recently noted:

> The assumption that there is an executive type is widely accepted, either openly or implicitly. Yet any executive presumably knows that a company needs all kinds of managers for different levels of jobs. The qualities most needed by a shop superintendent are likely to be quite opposed to those needed by a coordinating vice president of manufacturing. The literature of executive development is loaded

with efforts to define the qualities needed by executives, and by themselves these sound quite rational. Few, for instance, would dispute the fact that a top manager needs good judgment, the ability to make decisions, the ability to win respect of others, and all the other well-worn phrases any management man could mention. But one has only to look at the successful managers in any company to see how enormously their particular qualities vary from any ideal list of executive virtues.[1]

Yet this quest for the executive stereotype has become so intense that many companies, in concentrating on certain specific traits or qualities, stand in danger of losing sight of their real concern: *what a man can accomplish*.

It is the purpose of this article to suggest what may be a more useful approach to the selection and development of administrators. This approach is based not on what good executives *are* (their innate traits and characteristics), but rather on what they *do* (the kinds of skills which they exhibit in carrying out their jobs effectively). As used here, a *skill* implies an ability which can be developed, not necessarily inborn, and which is manifested in performance, not merely in potential. So the principal criterion of skillfulness must be effective action under varying conditions.

This approach suggests that effective administration rests on *three basic developable skills* which obviate the need for identifying specific traits and which may provide a useful way of looking at and understanding the administrative process. This approach is the outgrowth of firsthand observation of executives at work coupled with study of current field research in administration.

In the sections which follow, an attempt will be made to define and demonstrate what these three skills are; to suggest that the relative importance of the three skills varies with the level of administrative responsibility; to present some of the implications of this variation for selection, training, and

promotion of executives; and to propose
ways of developing these skills.

THREE-SKILL APPROACH

It is assumed here that an administrator is
one who (a) directs the activities of other
persons and (b) undertakes the responsibility for achieving certain objectives through
these efforts. Within this definition, successful administration appears to rest
on three basic skills, which we will call
technical, human, and *conceptual*. It would
be unrealistic to assert that these skills are
not interrelated, yet there may be real merit in
examining each one separately, and in developing them independently.

Technical Skill

As used here, technical skill implies an understanding of, and proficiency in, a specific kind of activity, particularly one involving methods, processes, procedures, or techniques. It is relatively easy for us to visualize the technical skill of the surgeon, the musician, the accountant, or the engineer when each is performing his own special function. Technical skill involves specialized knowledge, analytical ability within that specialty, and facility in the use of the tools and techniques of the specific discipline.

Of the three skills described in this article, technical skill is perhaps the most familiar because it is the most concrete, and because, in our age of specialization, it is the skill required of the greatest number of people. Most of our vocational and on-the-job training programs are largely concerned with developing this specialized technical skill.

Human Skill

As used here, human skill is the executive's ability to work effectively as a group member and to build cooperative effort within the team he leads. As *technical* skill is primarily concerned with working with "things" (processes or physical objects), so *human* skill is primarily concerned with working with people. This skill is demonstrated in the way the individual perceives (and recognizes the perceptions of) his superiors, equals, and subordinates, and in the way he behaves subsequently.

The person with highly developed human skill is aware of his own attitudes, assumptions, and beliefs about other individuals and groups; he is able to see the usefulness and limitations of these feelings. By accepting the existence of viewpoints, perceptions, and beliefs which are different from his own, he is skilled in understanding what others really mean by their words and behavior. He is equally skillful in communicating to others, in their own contexts, what he means by *his* behavior.

Such a person works to create an atmosphere of approval and security in which

subordinates feel free to express themselves
without fear of censure or ridicule, by
encouraging them to participate in the
planning and carrying out of those things
which directly affect them. He is sufficiently
sensitive to the needs and motivations of
others in his organization so that he can
judge the possible reactions to, and out-
comes of, various courses of action he
may undertake. Having this sensitivity, he
is able and willing to *act* in a way which
takes these perceptions by others into
account.

Real skill in working with others must
become a natural, continuous activity, since
it involves sensitivity not only at times of
decision making but also in the day-by-day

behavior of the individual. Human skill cannot be a "sometime thing." Techniques cannot be randomly applied, nor can personality traits be put on or removed like an overcoat. Because everything which an executive says and does (or leaves unsaid or undone) has an effect on his associates, his true self will, in time, show through. Thus, to be effective, this skill must be naturally developed and unconsciously, as well as consistently, demonstrated in the individual's every action. It must become an integral part of his whole being.

Because human skill is so vital a part of everything the administrator does, examples of inadequate human skill are easier to describe than are highly skillful performances.

Perhaps consideration of an actual situation would serve to clarify what is involved:

When a new conveyor unit was installed in a shoe factory where workers had previously been free to determine their own work rate, the production manager asked the industrial engineer who had designed the conveyor to serve as foreman, even though a qualified foreman was available. The engineer, who reported directly to the production manager, objected, but under pressure he agreed to take the job "until a suitable foreman could be found," even though this was a job of lower status than his present one. Then this conversation took place.

Production Manager: "I've had a lot of experience with conveyors. I want you to keep this conveyor going at all times except for rest periods, and I want it going at top speed. Get these people thinking in terms of 2 pairs of shoes a minute, 70 dozen pairs a day, 350 dozen pairs a week. They are all experienced operators on their individual jobs, and it's just a matter of getting them to do their jobs in a little different way. I want you to make that base rate of 250 dozen pair a week work!" [Base rate was established at slightly under 75% of the maximum capacity. This base rate was 50% higher than under the old system.]

Engineer: If I'm going to be foreman of the conveyor unit, I want to do things my way. I've worked on conveyors, and

I don't agree with you on first getting people used to a conveyor going at top speed.

These people have never seen a conveyor. You'll scare them. I'd like to run the conveyor at one-third speed for a couple of weeks and then gradually increase the speed.

I think we should discuss setting the base rate [production quota before incentive bonus] on a daily basis instead of a weekly basis. [Workers had previously been paid on a daily straight piecework basis.]

I'd also suggest setting a daily base rate at 45 or even 40 dozen pair. You have to set a base rate low enough for them to make. Once they know they can make the base rate, they will go after the bonus.

Production manager: You do it your way on the speed; but remember it's the results that count. On the base rate, I'm not discussing it with you; I'm telling you to make the 250 dozen pair a week work. I don't want a daily base rate.[2]

Here is a situation in which the production manager was so preoccupied with getting the physical output that he did not pay attention to the people through whom that output had to be achieved. Notice, first, that he made the engineer who designed the unit serve as foreman, apparently hoping to force the engineer to justify his design by producing the maximum output. However, the production manager was oblivious to (a) the way the engineer perceived this appointment, as a demotion, and (b) the need for the engineer to be able to control the variables if he was to be held responsible for maximum output. Instead the production manager imposed a production standard and refused to make any changes in the work situation.

Moreover, although this was a radically new situation for the operators, the production manager expected them to produce immediately at well above their previous output—even though the operators had an unfamiliar production system to cope with, the operators had never worked together as a team before, the operators and their new foreman had never worked together before, and the foreman was not in agreement with the production goals or standards. By ignoring all these human factors, the production manager not only placed the engineer in an extremely difficult operating situation but also, by refusing to allow the engineer to "run his own show," discouraged the very assumption of responsibility he had hoped for in making the appointment.

Under these circumstances, it is easy to understand how the relationship between these two men rapidly deteriorated, and how production, after two months' operation, was at only 125 dozen pairs per week (just

75% of what the output had been under the old system).

Conceptual Skill

As used here, conceptual skill involves the ability to see the enterprise as a whole; it includes recognizing how the various functions of the organization depend on one another, and how changes in any one part affect all the others; and it extends to visualizing the relationship of the individual business to the industry, the community, and the political, social, and economic forces of the nation as a whole. Recognizing these relationships and perceiving the significant elements in any situation, the administrator should then be able to act in a way which advances the over-all welfare of the total organization.

Hence, the success of any decision depends on the conceptual skill of the people who make the decision and those who put it into action. When, for example, an important change in marketing policy is made, it is critical that the effects on production, control, finance, research, and the people involved be considered. And it remains critical right down to the last executive who must implement the new policy. If each executive recognizes the over-all relationships and significance of the change, he is almost certain to be more effective in administering it. Consequently the chances for succeeding are greatly increased.

Not only does the effective coordination of the various parts of the business depend on the conceptual skill of the administrators involved, but so also does the whole future direction and tone of the organization. The attitudes of a top executive color the whole character of the organization's response and determine the "corporate personality" which distinguishes one company's ways of doing business from another's. These attitudes are a reflection of the administrator's conceptual skill (referred to by some as his "creative ability")—the way he perceives and responds to the direction in which the business should grow, company objectives and policies, and stockholders' and employees' interests.

Conceptual skill, as defined above, is what Chester I. Barnard, former president of the New Jersey Bell Telephone Company, is implying when he says: ". . . the essential aspect of the [executive] process is the sensing of the organization as a whole and of the total situation relevant to it."[3] Examples of inadequate conceptual skill are all around us. Here is one instance.

In a large manufacturing company which had a long tradition of job-shop type operations, primary responsibility for production control had been left to the foremen and other lower-level supervisors. "Village" type operations with small working groups and informal organizations were the rule. A heavy influx of orders following World War II tripled the normal production requirements and severely taxed the whole manufacturing organization. At this point, a new production manager was brought in from outside the company, and he established a wide range of controls and formalized the entire operating structure.

As long as the boom demand lasted, the employees made every effort to conform with the new procedures and environment. But when demand subsided to prewar levels, serious labor relations problems developed, friction was high among department heads, and the company found itself saddled with a heavy indirect labor cost. Management sought to reinstate its old procedures; it fired the production manager and attempted to give greater authority to the foremen once again. However, during the four years of formalized control, the foremen had grown away from their old practices, many had left the company, and adequate replacements had not been developed. Without strong foreman leadership, the traditional job-shop operations proved costly and inefficient.

In this instance, when the new production controls and formalized organizations were introduced, management did not foresee the consequences of this action in the event of a future contraction of business. Later, when conditions changed and it was necessary to pare down operations, management was again unable to recognize the implications of its action and reverted to the old procedures, which, under the circumstances, were no longer appropriate. This compounded conceptual inadequacy left the company at a serious competitive disadvantage.

Because a company's over-all success is dependent on its executives' conceptual skill in establishing and carrying out policy decisions, this skill is the unifying, coordinating ingredient of the administrative process, and of undeniable over-all importance.

RELATIVE IMPORTANCE

We may notice that, in a very real sense, conceptual skill embodies consideration of both the technical and human aspects of the organization. Yet the concept of *skill,* as an ability to translate knowledge into action, should enable one to distinguish between the three skills of performing the technical activities (technical skill), understanding and motivating individuals and groups (human skill), and coordinating and integrating all the activities and interests of the organization toward a common objective (conceptual skill).

This separation of effective administration into three basic skills is useful primarily for purposes of analysis. In practice, these skills are so closely interrelated that it is difficult to determine where one ends and another begins. However, just because the skills are interrelated does not imply that we cannot get some value from looking at them separately, or by varying their emphasis. In playing golf the action of the hands, wrists, hips, shoulders, arms, and head are all interrelated; yet in improving one's swing it is often valuable to work on one of these elements separately. Also, under different playing conditions the relative importance of these elements varies. Similarly, although all three are of importance at every level of administration, the technical, human, and conceptual skills of the administrator vary in relative importance at different levels of responsibility.

At Lower Levels

Technical skill is responsible for many of the great advances of modern industry. It is indispensable to efficient operation. Yet it has greatest importance at the lower levels of administration. As the administrator moves further and further from the actual physical operation, this need for technical skill becomes less important, provided he has skilled subordinates and can help them solve their own problems. At the top, technical skill may be almost nonexistent, and the executive may still be able to perform effectively if his human and conceptual skills are highly developed. For example, in one large capital-goods producing company, the controller was called on to replace the manufacturing vice president, who had been stricken suddenly with a severe illness. The controller had no previous production experience, but he had been with the company for more than 20 years and knew many of the key production personnel intimately. By setting up an advisory staff, and by delegating an unusual amount of authority to his department heads, he was able to devote himself to coordination of the various functions. By so doing, he produced a highly efficient team. The results were lower costs, greater productivity, and higher morale than the production division had ever before experienced. Management had gambled that this man's ability to work with people was more important than his lack of a technical production background, and the gamble paid off.

Other examples are evident all around us. We are all familiar with those "professional managers" who are becoming the prototypes of our modern executive world. These men shift with great ease, and with no apparent loss in effectiveness, from one industry to another. Their human and conceptual skills seem to make up for their unfamiliarity with the new job's technical aspects.

At Every Level

Human skill, the ability to work with others, is essential to effective administration at every level. One recent research study has shown that human skill is of paramount importance at the foreman level, pointing out that the chief function of the foreman as an administrator is to attain collaboration of people in the work group.[4] Another study reinforces this finding and extends it to the middle-management group, adding that the administrator should be primarily concerned with facilitating communication in the organization.[5] And still another study, concerned primarily with top management, underscores the need for self-awareness and sensitivity to human relationships by executives at that level.[6] These findings would tend to indicate that human skill is of great importance at every level, but notice the difference in emphasis.

Human skill seems to be most important at lower levels, where the number of direct contacts between administrators and subordinates is greatest. As we go higher and higher in the administrative echelons, the number and frequency of these personal contacts decrease, and the need for human skill becomes proportionately, although probably not absolutely, less. At the same time, conceptual skill becomes increasingly more important with the need for policy decisions and broad-scale action. The human skill of dealing with individuals then becomes subordinate to the conceptual skill of integrating group interests and activities into a whole.

In fact, a recent research study by Professor Chris Argyris of Yale University has given us the example of an extremely effective plant manager who, although possessing little human skill as defined here, was nonetheless very successful:

> This manager, the head of a largely autonomous division, made his supervisors, through the effects of his strong

personality and the "pressure" he applied, highly dependent on him for most of their "rewards, penalties, authority, perpetuation, communication, and identification.

As a result, the supervisors spent much of their time competing with one another for the manager's favor. They told him only the things they thought he wanted to hear, and spent much time trying to find out his desires. They depended on him to set their objectives and to show them how to reach them. Because the manager was inconsistent and unpredictable in his behavior, the supervisors were insecure and continually engaged in interdepartmental squabbles which they tried to keep hidden from the manager.

Clearly, human skill as defined here was lacking. Yet, by the evaluation of his superiors and by his results in increasing efficiency and raising profits and morale, this manager was exceedingly effective. Professor Argyris suggests that employees in modern industrial organizations tend to have a "built-in" sense of dependence on superiors which capable and alert men can turn to advantage.[7]

In the context of the three-skill approach, it seems that this manager was able to capitalize on this dependence because he recognized the interrelationships of all the activities under his control, identified himself with the organization, and sublimated the individual interests of his subordinates to *his* (the organization's) interest, set his goals realistically, and showed his subordinates how to reach these goals. This would seem to be an excellent example of a situation in which strong conceptual skill more than compensated for a lack of human skill.

At the Top Level

Conceptual skill, as indicated in the preceding sections, becomes increasingly critical in more responsible executive positions where its effects are maximized and most easily observed. In fact, recent research findings lead to the conclusion that at the top level of administration this conceptual skill becomes the most important ability of all. As Herman W. Steinkraus, president of Bridgeport Brass Company, said:

> One of the most important lessons which I learned on this job [the presidency] is the importance of coordinating the various departments into an effective team, and, secondly, to recognize the shifting emphasis from time to time of the relative importance of various departments to the business.[8]

It would appear, then, that at lower levels of administrative responsibility, the principal need is for technical and human skills. At higher levels, technical skill becomes relatively less important while the need for conceptual skill increases rapidly. At the top level of an organization, conceptual skill becomes the most important skill of all for successful administration. A chief executive may lack technical or human skills and still be effective if he has subordinates who have strong abilities in these directions. But if his conceptual skill is weak, the success of the whole organization may be jeopardized.

IMPLICATIONS FOR ACTION

This three-skill approach implies that significant benefits may result from redefining the objectives of executive development programs, from reconsidering the placement of executives in organizations, and from revising procedures for testing and selecting prospective executives.

Executive Development

Many executive development programs may be failing to achieve satisfactory results because of their inability to foster the growth of these administrative skills. Programs which concentrate on the mere imparting of information or the cultivation of a specific trait would seem to be largely unproductive in enhancing the administrative skills of candidates.

A strictly informative program was described to me recently by an officer and director of a large corporation who had been responsible for the executive-development activities of his company, as follows:

> What we try to do is to get our promising young men together with some of our senior executives in regular meetings each month. Then we give the young fellows a chance to ask questions to let them find out about the company's history and how and why we've done things in the past.

It was not surprising that neither the senior executives nor the young men felt this program was improving their administrative abilities.

The futility of pursuing specific traits becomes apparent when we consider the responses of an administrator in a number of different situations. In coping with these varied conditions, he may appear to demonstrate one trait in one instance—e.g., dominance when dealing with subordinates—and the directly opposite trait under another set of circumstances—e.g., submissiveness when dealing with superiors. Yet in each instance he may be acting appropriately to achieve the best results. Which, then, can we identify as a desirable characteristic? Here is a further example of this dilemma. A Pacific Coast sales manager had a reputation for decisiveness and positive action. Yet when he was required to name an assistant to understudy his job from among several well-qualified subordinates, he deliberately avoided making a decision. His associates were quick to observe what appeared to be obvious indecisiveness.

But after several months had passed, it became clear that the sales manager had very unobtrusively been giving the various salesmen opportunities to demonstrate their attitudes and feelings. As a result, he was able to identify strong sentiments for one man whose subsequent promotion was enthusiastically accepted by the entire group.

In this instance, the sales manager's skillful performance was improperly interpreted as "indecisiveness." Their concern with irrelevant traits led his associates to overlook the adequacy of his performance. Would it not have been more appropriate to conclude that his human skill in working with others enabled him to adapt effectively to the requirements of a new situation?

Cases such as these would indicate that it is more useful to judge an administrator on the results of his performance than on his apparent traits. Skills are easier to identify than are traits and are less likely to be misinterpreted. Furthermore, skills offer a more directly applicable frame of reference for executive development, since any improvement in an administrator's skills must necessarily result in more effective performance.

Still another danger in many existing executive development programs lies in the unqualified enthusiasm with which some companies and colleges have embraced courses in "human relations." There would seem to be two inherent pitfalls here: (1) Human relations courses might only be imparting information or specific techniques, rather than developing the individual's human skill. (2) Even if individual development does take place, some companies, by placing all of their emphasis on human skill, may be completely overlooking the training requirements for top positions. They may run the risk of producing men with highly developed human skill who lack the conceptual ability to be effective top-level administrators.

It would appear important, then, that the training of a candidate for an administrative position be directed at the development of those skills which are most needed at the level of responsibility for which he is being considered.

Executive Placement

This three-skill concept suggests immediate possibilities for the creating of management teams of individuals with complementary skills. For example, one medium-size midwestern distributing organization has as president a man of unusual conceptual ability but extremely limited human skill. However, he has two vice presidents with exceptional human skill. These three men make up an executive committee which has been outstandingly successful, the skills of each member making

{ 43 }

up for deficiencies of the others. Perhaps the plan of two-man complementary conference leadership proposed by Robert F. Bales, in which the one leader maintains "task leadership" while the other provides "social leadership," might also be an example in point.[9]

Executive Selection

In trying to predetermine a prospective candidate's abilities on a job, much use is being made these days of various kinds of testing devices. Executives are being tested for everything from "decisiveness" to "conformity." These tests, as a recent article in *Fortune* points out, have achieved some highly questionable results when applied to performance on the job.[10] Would it not be much more productive to be concerned with skills of doing rather than with a number of traits which do not guarantee performance?

This three-skill approach makes trait testing unnecessary and substitutes for it procedures which examine a man's ability to cope with the actual problems and situations he will find on his job. These procedures, which indicate what a man can *do* in specific situations, are the same for selection and for measuring development. They will be described in the section on developing executive skills which follows.

This approach suggests that executives should *not* be chosen on the basis of their apparent possession of a number of behavior characteristics or traits, but on the basis of their possession of the requisite skills for the specific level of responsibility involved.

DEVELOPING THE SKILLS

For years many people have contended that leadership ability is inherent in certain chosen individuals. We talk of "born leaders," "born executives," "born salesmen." It is undoubtedly true that certain people, naturally or innately, possess greater aptitude or ability in certain skills. But research in psychology and physiology would also indicate, first, that those having strong aptitudes and abilities can improve their skill through practice and training, and, secondly, that even those lacking the natural ability can improve their performance and over-all effectiveness.

The *skill* conception of administration suggests that we may hope to improve our administrative effectiveness and to develop better administrators for the future. This skill conception implies *learning by doing.* Different people learn in different ways, but skills are developed through practice and through relating learning to one's own personal experience and background. If well done, training in these basic administrative skills should develop executive abilities more surely and more rapidly than through unorganized experience. What, then, are some of the ways in which this training can be conducted?

Technical Skill

Development of technical skill has received great attention for many years by industry and educational institutions alike, and much progress has been made. Sound grounding in the principles, structures, and processes of the individual specialty, coupled with actual practice and experience during which the individual is watched and helped by a superior, appear to be most effective. In view of the vast amount of work which has been done in training people in the technical skills, it would seem unnecessary in this article to suggest more.

Human Skill

Human skill, however, has been much less understood, and only recently has systematic progress been made in developing it. Many different approaches to the development of human skill are being pursued by various universities and professional men today. These are rooted in such disciplines as psychology, sociology, and anthropology.

Some of these approaches find their application in "applied psychology," "human engineering," and a host of other manifestations requiring technical specialists to help the businessman with his human problems. As a practical matter, however, the executive must develop his own human skill, rather than lean on the advice of others. To be effective, he must develop his own personal point of view toward human activity, so that he will (a) recognize the feelings and sentiments which he brings to a situation; (b) have an attitude about his own experiences which will enable him to re-evaluate and learn from them; (c) develop ability in understanding what others by their actions and words (explicit or implicit) are trying to communicate to him; and (d) develop ability in successfully communicating his ideas and attitudes to others.[11]

This human skill can be developed by some individuals without formalized training. Others can be individually aided by their immediate superiors as an integral part of the "coaching" process to be described later. This aid depends for effectiveness, obviously, on the extent to which the superior possesses the human skill.

For larger groups, the use of case problems coupled with impromptu role playing can be very effective. This training can be established on a formal or informal basis, but it requires a skilled instructor and organized sequence of activities.[12] It affords as good an approximation to reality as can be provided on a continuing classroom basis and offers an opportunity for critical reflection not often found in actual practice. An important part of the procedure is the self-examination of the trainee's own concepts and values, which may enable him to develop more useful attitudes about himself and about others. With the change in attitude, hopefully, there may also come some active skill in dealing with human problems.

Human skill has also been tested in the classroom, within reasonable limits, by a series of analyses of detailed accounts of actual situations involving administrative action, together with a number of role-playing opportunities in which the individual is required to carry out the details of the action he has proposed. In this way an individual's understanding of the total situation and his own personal ability to do something about it can be evaluated.

On the job, there should be frequent opportunities for a superior to observe an individual's ability to work effectively with others. These may appear to be highly subjective evaluations and to depend for validity on the human skill of the rater. But does not every promotion, in the last analysis, depend on someone's subjective judgment? And should this subjectivity be berated, or should we make a greater effort to develop people within our organizations with the human skill to make such judgments effectively?

Conceptual Skill

Conceptual skill, like human skill, has not been very widely understood. A number of methods have been tried to aid in developing this ability, with varying success. Some of the best results have always been achieved through the "coaching" of subordinates by superiors.[13] This is no new idea. It implies that one of the key responsibilities of the executive is to help his subordinates to develop their administrative potentials. One way a superior can help "coach" his subordinate is by assigning a particular responsibility, and then responding with searching questions or opinions, rather than giving answers, whenever the subordinate seeks help. When Benjamin F. Fairless, now chairman of the board of the United States Steel Corporation, was president of the corporation, he described his coaching activities:

> When one of my vice presidents or the head of one of our operating companies comes to me for instructions, I generally counter by asking him questions. First thing I know, he has told me how to solve the problem himself.[14]

Obviously, this is an ideal and wholly natural procedure for administrative training, and applies to the development of technical and human skill, as well as to that of conceptual skill. However, its success must necessarily rest on the abilities and willingness of the superior to help the subordinate.

Another excellent way to develop conceptual skill is through trading jobs, that is, by moving promising young men through different functions of the business but at the same level of responsibility. This gives the man the chance literally to "be in the other fellow's shoes."

Other possibilities include: special assignments, particularly the kind which involve inter-departmental problems; and management boards, such as the McCormick Multiple Management plan, in which junior executives serve as advisers to top management on policy matters.

For larger groups, the kind of case-problems course described above, only using cases involving broad management policy and interdepartmental coordination, may be useful. Courses of this kind, often called "General Management" or "Business Policy," are becoming increasingly prevalent.

In the classroom, conceptual skill has also been evaluated with reasonable effectiveness by presenting a series of detailed descriptions of specific complex situations. In these the individual being tested is asked to set forth a course of action which responds to the underlying forces operating in each situation and which considers the implications of this action on the various functions and parts of the organization and its total environment.

On the job, the alert supervisor should find frequent opportunities to observe the extent to which the individual is able to relate himself and his job to the other functions and operations of the company.

Like human skill, conceptual skill, too, must become a natural part of the executive's makeup. Different methods may be indicated for developing different people, by virtue of their backgrounds, attitudes, and experience. But in every case that method should be chosen which will enable the executive to develop his own personal skill in visualizing the enterprise as a whole and in coordinating and integrating its various parts.

CONCLUSION

The purpose of this article has been to show that effective administration depends on three basic personal skills, which have been called *technical, human,* and *conceptual.* The administrator needs: (a) sufficient technical skill to accomplish the mechanics of the particular job for which he is responsible; (b) sufficient human skill in working with others to be an effective group member and to be able to build cooperative effort within the team he leads; (c) sufficient conceptual skill to recognize the interrelationships of the various factors involved in his situation, which will lead him to take that action which is likely to achieve the maximum good for the total organization.

The relative importance of these three skills seems to vary with the level of administrative responsibility. At lower levels, the major need is for technical and human skills. At higher levels, the administrator's effectiveness depends largely on human and conceptual skills. At the top, conceptual skill becomes the most important of all for successful administration.

This three-skill approach emphasizes that good administrators are not necessarily born; they may be developed. It transcends the need to identify specific traits in an effort to provide a more useful way of looking at the administrative process. By helping to identify the skills most needed at various levels of responsibility, it may prove useful in the selection, training, and promotion of executives.

Retrospective Commentary

When this article was first published nearly 20 years ago, there was a great deal of interest in trying to identify a set of ideal personality traits that would readily distinguish potential executive talent. The search for these traits was vigorously pursued in the hope that the selection and training of managers could be conducted with greater reliability.

This article was an attempt to focus attention on demonstrable skills of performance rather than on innate personality characteristics. And, while describing the three kinds of administrative skill (technical, human, and conceptual), it also attempted to highlight the importance of conceptual skill as a uniquely valuable managerial capability, long before the concept of corporate strategy was well defined or popularly understood.

It still appears useful to think of managerial ability in terms of these three basic, observable skills. It also still appears that the relative importance of these skills varies with the administrative level of the manager in the organization. However, my experience over the past 20 years, in working with senior executives in a wide variety of industries, suggests that several specific points require either sharp modification or substantial further refinement.

Human Skill

I now believe that this kind of skill could be usefully subdivided into (a) leadership ability within the manager's own unit and (b) skill in intergroup relationships. In my experience, outstanding capability in one of these roles is frequently accompanied by mediocre performance in the other.

Often, the most internally efficient department managers are those who have committed themselves fully to the unique values and criteria of their specialized functions, without acknowledging that other departments' differing values have any validity at all. For example, a production manager may be most efficient if he puts all his emphasis on obtaining a high degree of reliability in his production schedule. He would then resist any external pressures that place a higher priority on criteria other than delivering the required output on time. Or a sales manager may be most efficient if he puts all his emphasis on maintaining positive relationships with customers. He would then resist all pressures that would emphasize other values, such as ease of production or selling the highest gross margin items. In each case, the manager will probably receive strong support from his subordinates, who share the same values. But he will encounter severe antagonism from other departments with conflicting values.

To the extent that two departments' values conflict with each other, skillful intergroup relationships require some equivocation. But compromise is often perceived by departmental subordinates as a "sellout." Thus the manager is obliged to choose between gaining full support from subordinates or enjoying full collaboration with peers and/or superiors. Having both is rarely possible. Consequently, I would revise my original evaluation of human skill to say now that internal *intragroup* skills are essential in lower and middle management roles and that *intergroup* skills become increasingly important in successively higher levels of management.

Conceptual Skill

In retrospect, I now see that what I called conceptual skill depends entirely on a specific way of thinking about an enterprise. This "general management point of view," as it has come to be known, involves always thinking in terms of the following: relative emphases and priorities among conflicting objectives and criteria; relative tendencies and probabilities (rather than certainties); rough correlations and patterns among elements (rather than clear-cut cause-and-effect relationships).

I am now far less sanguine about the degree to which this way of thinking can be developed on the job. Unless a person has learned to think this way early in life, it is unrealistic to expect a major change on reaching executive status. Job rotation, special interdepartmental assignments, and working with case problems certainly provide opportunities for a person to enhance previously developed conceptual abilities. But I question how easily this way of thinking can be inculcated after a person passes adolescence. In this sense, then, conceptual skill should perhaps be viewed as an innate ability.

Technical Skill

In the original article, I suggested that specific technical skills are unimportant at top management levels. I cited as evidence the many professional managers who move easily from one industry to another without apparent loss of effectiveness.

I now believe this mobility is possible only in very large companies, where the chief executive has extensive staff assistance and highly competent, experienced technical operators throughout the organization. An old, established, large company has great operational momentum that enables the new chief executive to concentrate on strategic issues.

In smaller companies, where technical expertise is not as pervasive and seasoned staff assistance is not as available, I believe the chief executive has a much greater need for personal experience in the industry. He not only needs to know the right questions to ask his subordinates; he also needs enough industry background to know how to evaluate the answers.

Role of the Chief Executive

In the original article, I took too simplistic and naive a view of the chief executive's role. My extensive work with company presidents and my own personal experience as a chief executive have given me much more respect for the difficulties and complexities of that role. I now know that every important executive action must strike a balance among so many conflicting values, objectives, and criteria that it will always be suboptimal from any single viewpoint. *Every* decision or choice affecting the whole enterprise has negative consequences for some of the parts.

The chief executive must try to perceive the conflicts and trace accurately their likely impact throughout the organization. Reluctantly, but wittingly, he may have to sacrifice the interests of a single unit or part for the good of the whole. He needs to be willing to accept solutions that are adequate and feasible in the total situation rather than what, from a single point of view, may be elegant or optimum.

Not only must the chief executive be an efficient operator, but he must also be an effective strategist. It is his responsibility to provide the framework and direction for overall company operations. He must continually specify where the company will place its emphasis in terms of products, services, and customers. He must define performance crite- ria and determine what special competences the company will emphasize. He also needs to set priorities and timetables. He must establish the standards and controls neces- sary to monitor progress and to place limits on individual actions. He must bring into the

enterprise additional resources when they are
needed.

Moreover, he must change his management
style and strike different balances among his
personal skills as conditions change or as his
organization grows in size and complexity. The
remedial role (saving the organization when it
is in great difficulty) calls for drastic human action and emphasizes conceptual and technical
skills. The *maintaining* role (sustaining the organization in its present posture) emphasizes
human skills and requires only modest technical or strategic changes. But the *innovative*
role (developing and expanding the organization) demands high competence in both
conceptual and intergroup skills, with the
technical contribution provided primarily
by subordinates.

{ 70 }

In my view, it is impossible for anyone to perform well in these continually changing roles without help. Yet because effective management of the total enterprise involves constant suboptimizing, it is impossible for the chief executive to get unanimous or continuous support from his subordinates. If he is overly friendly or supportive, he may compromise his effectiveness or his objectivity. Yet somewhere in the organization, he needs to have a well-informed, objective, understanding, and supportive sounding board with whom he can freely discuss his doubts, fears, and aspirations. Sometimes this function can be supplied by an outside director, the outside corporate counsel, or the company auditor. But such a confidant requires just as high a degree of conceptual and human skills as the chief executive himself; and to be truly helpful, he must know all about the company's operations, key personnel, and industry. This role has been largely overlooked in discussions of organizational requirements, but in my view, its proper fulfillment is essential to the success of the chief executive and the enterprise.

Conclusion

I now realize more fully that managers at all levels require some competence in each of the three skills. Even managers at the lowest levels must continually use all of them. Dealing with the external demands on a manager's unit requires conceptual skill; the limited physical and financial resources available to him tax his technical skill; and the capabilities and demands of the persons with whom he deals make it essential that he possess human skill. A clear idea of these skills and of ways to measure a manager's competence in each category still appears to me to be a most effective tool for top management, not only in understanding executive behavior, but also in the selection, training, and promotion of managers at all levels.

NOTES

1. Perrin Stryker, "The Growing Pains of Executive Development," *Advanced Management,* August 1954, p. 15.

2. From a mimeographed case in the files of the Harvard Business School; copyrighted by the President and Fellows of Harvard College.

3. *Functions of the Executive* (Cambridge, Harvard University Press, 1948), p. 235.

4. A. Zaleznik, *Foreman Training in a Growing Enterprise* (Boston, Division of Research, Harvard Business School, 1951).

5. Harriet O. Ronken and Paul R. Lawrence, *Administering Changes* (Boston, Division of Research, Harvard Business School, 1952).

6. Edmund P. Learned, David H. Ulrich, and Donald R. Booz, *Executive Action* (Boston, Division of Research, Harvard Business School, 1950).

7. *Executive Leadership* (New York, Harper & Brothers, 1953); see also "Leadership Pattern in the Plant," HBR January–February 1954, p. 63.

8. "What Should a President Do?" *Dun's Review,* August 1951, p. 21.

9. "In Conference," HBR March-April 1954, p. 44.

10. William H. Whyte, Jr., "The Fallacies of 'Personality' Testing," *Fortune,* September 1954, p. 117.

11. For a further discussion of this point, see F. J. Roethlisberger, "Training Supervisors in Human Relations," HBR September 1951, p. 47.

12. See, for example, A. Winn, "Training in Administration and Human Relations," *Personnel,* September 1953, p. 139; see also, Kenneth R. Andrews, "Executive Training by the Case Method," HBR September 1951, p. 58.

13. For a more comlete development of the concept of "coaching," see Myles L. Mace, The Growth and Development of Executives (Boston, Division of Research, Harvard Business School, 1950).

14. "What Should a President Do?" Dun's Review, July 1951, p. 14.

ABOUT THIS AUTHOR

At the time this article was written, Robert
L. Katz was assistant professor at the Amos
Tuck School of Business Administration,
Dartmouth College. Since then he has
taught in the graduate schools of business
at Harvard and Stanford, written three
textbooks, and helped found five industrial
or financial companies.